1 New London Bridge, seen from the watermen's stairs at Tooley Street on the south bank of the river. Opened by the City Corporation in 1831, the bridge was designed by John Rennie. (right)

Front and back covers

Details from the two middle sections of the 'Rhinebeck' watercolour panorama of London, around 1810. Even after the opening of London's early docks, to the east of the Tower, coastal and European shipping still crowded into the Upper Pool. All manner of smaller craft – such as lighters, sailing barges, hoys, skiffs, wherries and ceremonial barges – added to the bustle of the river.

London's historic river port centred on the City waterfront, between London Bridge and the Tower (front cover). This area had been the focus of port activity in Roman and medieval times. Between the 1550s and the building of the docks, most dutiable cargoes coming into the port had to be landed at the twenty Legal Quays which operated here. On the Bermondsey waterfront (back cover) eighteenth-century Sufferance Wharves stand on the sites of what had once been medieval granaries.

Compiled by different artists, this watercolour, with its high vantage-point and exaggerated buildings, was almost certainly designed as the artwork for a large scale panorama of the type which entertained Londoners at the Panorama in Leicester Square.

COURTESY THE OWNER

Inside front cover (left)

Detail of Canaletto's painting of the Thames on Lord Mayor's Day, about 1747. The City barge appears immediately behind the sloop firing a salute. Four livery company barges can also be seen heading upriver to Westminster, accompanied by a large array of watermen's wherries. The City waterfront, seen here from Puddle Dock to Brook's Wharf, was lined with working warehouses.

COURTESY ROYLE PUBLICATIONS LIMITED

THE MUSEUM OF LONDON 1989

The Museum of London is funded jointly by the Office of Arts & Libraries and the Corporation of the City of London

Text by Chris Ellmers
Edited by Caroline Williamson
Photography by John Edwards, Torla Evans, Barrington Gray, Nick Lane, Marcus Leith and Richard Stroud
Designed by David Milbank Challis
Printed in England by Balding & Mansell Limited, Wisbech
ISBN 0 904818 29 2

CITY & RIVER

The long and rich association between the City Corporation and London's river dates back to the late twelfth century, when the Mayor was granted conservancy powers for the Thames. Over the centuries this association was to extend to encompass most of the activities of the busy Port of London.

Under its various charters, the City Corporation levied duties on a wide range of river-borne trade and controlled the activities of most portworkers. This involvement provided the City and the Mayor with much of their power and influence, which, uniquely, extended way beyond the limits of the 'square mile'. As Alexander Pulling, the legal historian of the Corporation, wrote in 1854, it was 'a subject which concerns not only the whole of the city, but affects, in a great degree, the commerce of the world'.

Lavish river ceremonials, which both the Corporation and the livery companies engaged in, provided outward shows of this wealth and power. As well as the Lord Mayor's annual procession to Westminster, there were all manner of royal and public occasions.

The City remained the conservancy body for the river until 1857, when it handed its powers over to the Thames Conservancy. The Corporation, however, retained an influence in this new body and the Mayor acted as its Chairman. In 1872 the City became responsible for the Port Health Service, which it still provides.

Up until 1800, City wharves and warehouses were the focus of London's working port and their activities provided the key to much of London's commercial and industrial success. Even after the opening of London's trading docks – in some of which the Corporation had a direct involvement – the City waterfront remained a hive of activity, the last cargo handling wharf surviving until the early 1980s.

2 *David Steel's 'Chart of the River Thames from London Bridge to Woolwich Warren', 1802 (detail). Few reliable charts were available to mariners before the late eighteenth century. Steel's chart provided valuable details of the depth of the river at low water, extent of the foreshore, direction of tidal flow, mooring chains and distances from London Bridge. Pilots and watermen, however, relied on their own practical knowledge when navigating shipping.*

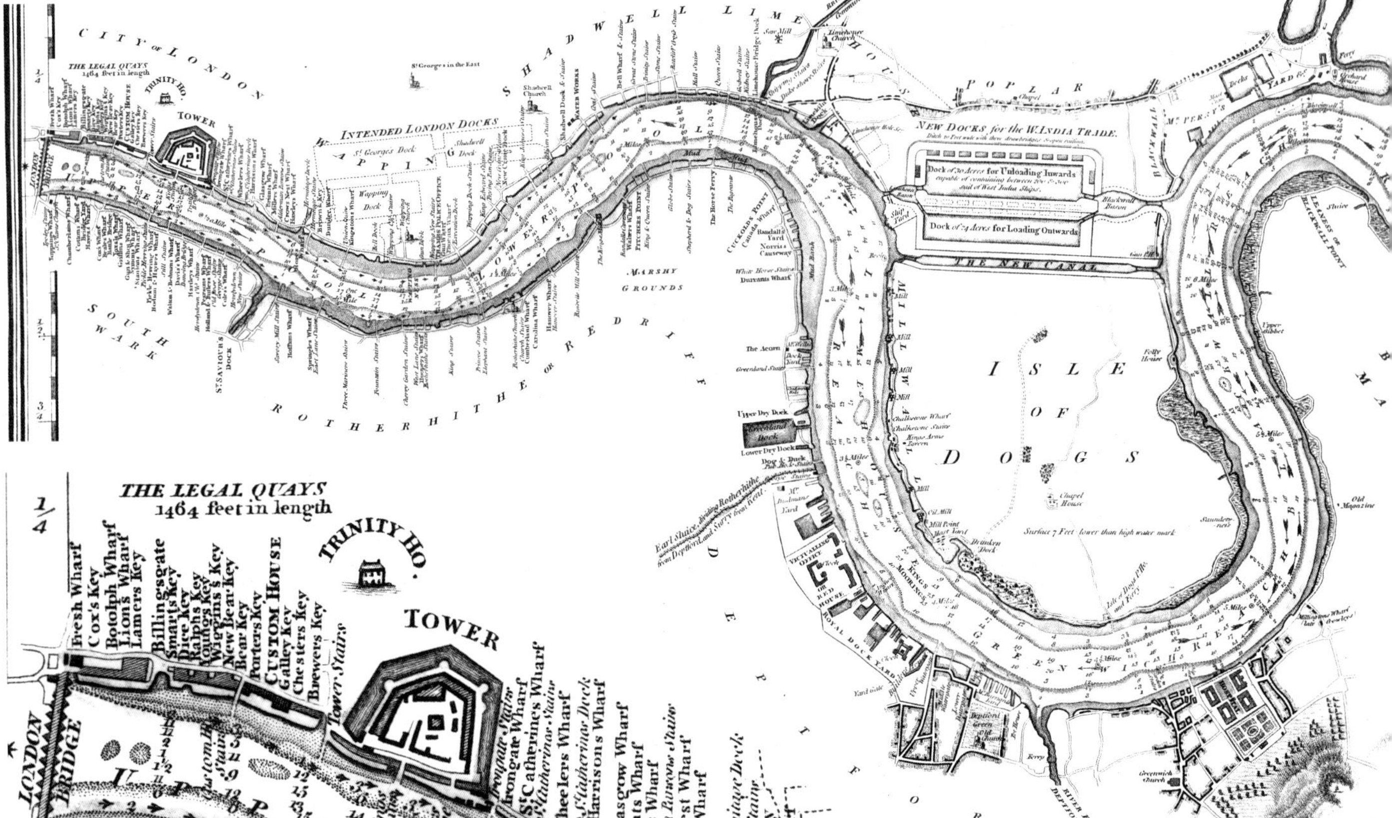

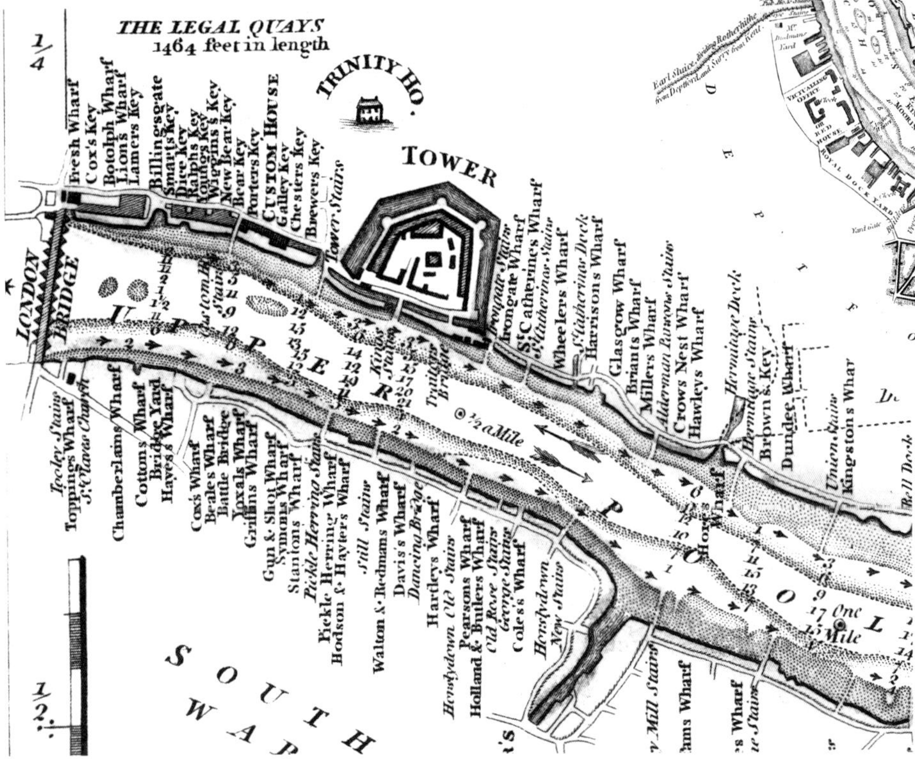

3 *The Upper Pool, from Steel's chart of 1802. This section of the river was crowded with ships, often lying six abreast at the mooring chains, waiting to transfer their cargoes to the busy quays. The movement and mooring of shipping was closely controlled by the Corporation's Harbour Masters.*

In 1189, according to tradition, Henry Fitz Ailwyn became the first Mayor of London. Eight years later Richard I granted a charter to the City which gave rights to remove fishing weirs. A statute of 1393 named the Mayor as Conservator of the Thames, from Staines Bridge to Yantlet Creek downriver (opposite the present-day Southend on Sea).

With the help of his Harbour Masters, River Bailiffs and special committees, the Mayor was responsible for maintaining quays, making causeways and stairs, laying mooring chains and charting the river. In 1857, these powers passed to the newly formed Thames Conservancy.

5 Hollar's view of the City waterfront, 1647. Old London Bridge provided a great hazard to navigation.

4 The 'Crow Stone' at Leigh-on-Sea, seen here in 1829, marked the eastern limit of the City's river jurisdiction. At Staines, some sixty-five miles upriver, the equally massive 'City Stone' marked the western boundary of authority. Somewhat surprisingly, Mayors and Aldermen were traditionally 'bumped' on these stones by City Watermen.

6 Low tide at Putney Bridge, 1793. The Corporation's River Bailiff was responsible for checking the state of the riverbank and for controlling the activities of fishermen, like those seen here long-netting for salmon. The City extracted valuable tolls from the 'west country barges' which traded upriver.

The City waterfront was the centre of port activity during the Roman and medieval periods. By Elizabethan times, City quaysides were alive with activity, enjoying the benefits of England's links with new parts of the world and its growing maritime power. In 1558, when London monopolised half of the nation's trade, twenty 'Legal Quays' were established, between London Bridge and the Tower, for the handling of cargoes and collection of customs dues.

During the eighteenth century, trade more than tripled as London became the world's busiest port. Supported by City financial institutions, commodity exchanges and insurance brokers, the quaysides and warehouses were full to overflowing. Imports provided for the needs of Londoners, and were re-exported to Europe and the colonies. The City levied rates on shipping and received valuable duties on wine, oil, coal, grain, salt, fish and fruit.

As the forest of masts in the Upper Pool grew, however, so too did the problems. By the 1790s chronic overcrowding and expensive delays, together with an alarming level of theft and dishonesty, had combined to threaten the very future of the port itself.

7 This animated 1757 scene of the Legal Quays shows the intense overcrowding in the port.

8 Surviving artefacts from the mid-eighteenth-century river port include this chain tackle, cargo hook, wharf handbill and Fellowship Porter's tally, or badge. (right)

9 Busy wharves and warehouses line the City waterfront, 1749. Those above London Bridge mostly handled grain, fruit, timber and coal. (below)

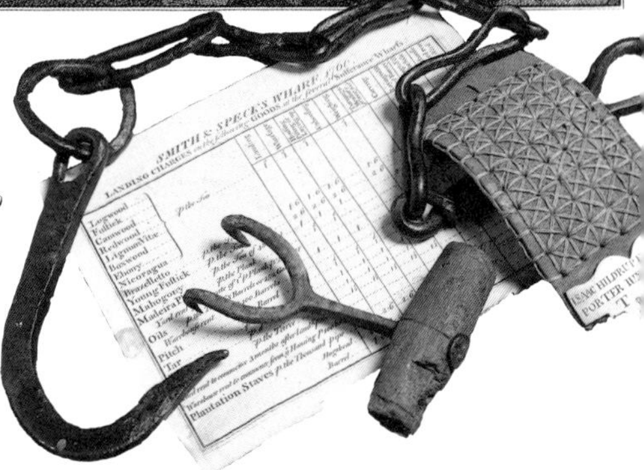

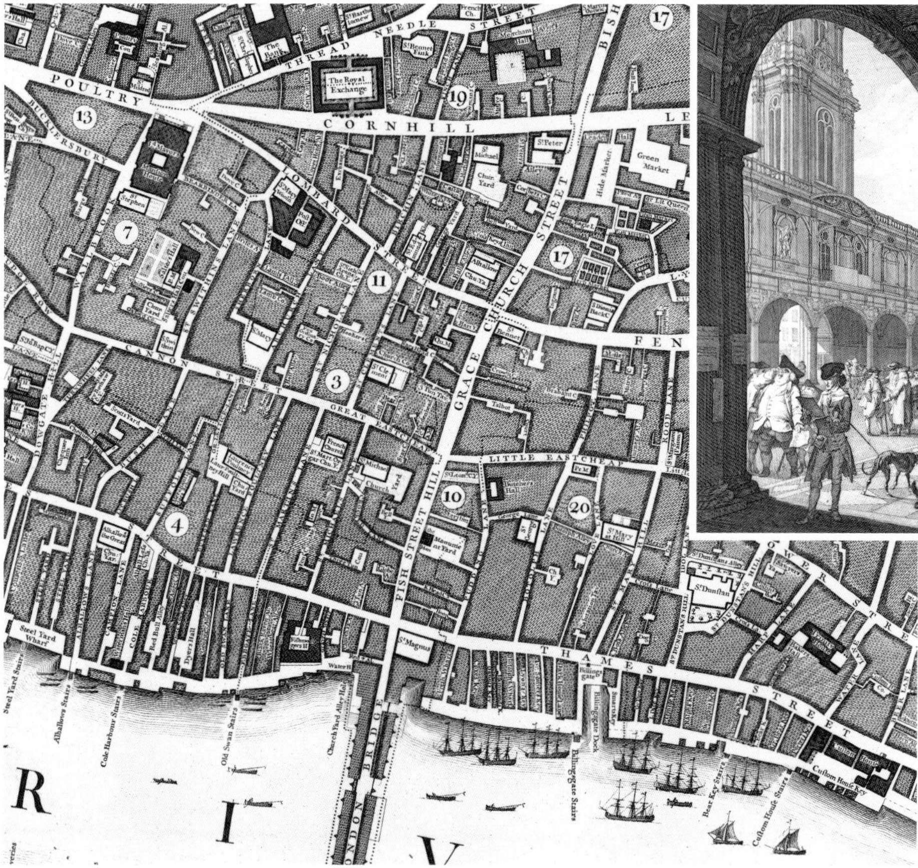

11 Merchants and insurance brokers about their business at the Royal Exchange in 1788. With the rapid growth of trade, however, an increasing number of traders moved their businesses to the specialist coffee houses around Cornhill. (above)

10 Detail from John Rocque's plan of 1746. The influence of the earlier medieval layout remained strong along the riverside, with its narrow building plots and alleyways. Along Thames Street were warehouses, cooperages and processing works, such as sugar refineries. (left)

As trade expanded, larger ships had to lay downriver at Limehouse, Deptford, Blackwall and Woolwich, where they transferred their cargoes into fleets of barges, which added to the bustle of the river. As the City Legal Quays became increasingly congested, the Government allowed 'Sufferance Wharves' to be built in Bermondsey and St Katharine's, for the handling of lower value dutiable cargoes.

Eastwards of the City, the riverside parishes also serviced the needs of London's sailors, and their riverfronts housed wharves, handling coal and grain, and ship-building yards. Here also were to be found the Greenland Dock, at Rotherhithe (opened around 1699), and the Brunswick Dock, at Blackwall (1790). Although both of these docks were designed for the fitting-out of ships, they also acted as Sufferance Wharves for the discharge of London whaling ships. Docks like these held the key to the future of the port.

By the mid-1790s merchants were petitioning Parliament for the building of new trading docks, downriver of the City. The City Corporation and the Legal Quay owners fought to retain their monopoly of trade, but this was shortlived, and the construction of the West India Docks soon began on the Poplar marshes.

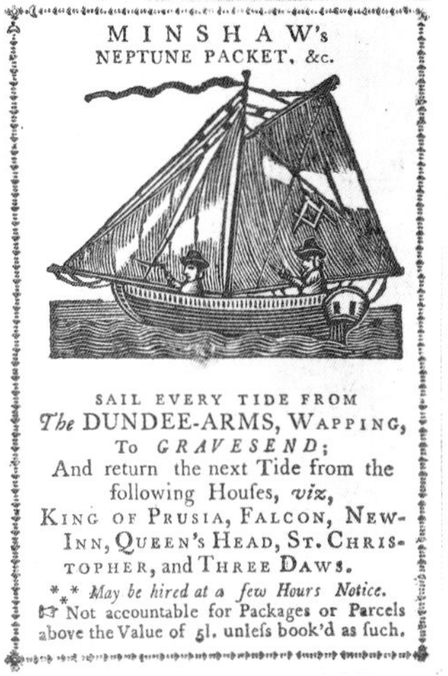

MINSHAW's
NEPTUNE PACKET, &c.

SAIL EVERY TIDE FROM
The DUNDEE-ARMS, WAPPING,
To *GRAVESEND*;
And return the next Tide from the
following Houſes, *viz,*
KING OF PRUSIA, FALCON, NEW-INN, QUEEN's HEAD, ST. CHRISTOPHER, and THREE DAWS.
*** *May be hired at a few Hours Notice.*
☞ Not accountable for Packages or Parcels above the Value of 5l. unleſs book'd as ſuch.

12 Advertisement for a London to Gravesend packet, late 1790s. The wharves of Wapping, Ratcliff, Shadwell, Limehouse, Bermondsey and Rotherhithe were heavily engaged in the coasting trade.

13 Careening a coaster at Rotherhithe. In the 1790s the Rotherhithe waterfront was mostly lined with shipyards and timber wharves.

14 John Perry's Brunswick Dock at Blackwall, looking east. Opened in 1790, the dock was chiefly intended for the accommodation and fitting-out of East India Company ships. The 120-foot high masthouse offered a welcome landmark for homeward bound sailors. (right)

15 View of shipping at Limehouse Reach, 1793, looking north-west from the top of the Isle of Dogs. Timber rafters are busy at work on the river.

16 The huge fleet of collier ships, which brought coal from the Northumberland and Durham coalfield, dominated London's coasting trade. From the early eighteenth century, the discharging of colliers gradually moved eastwards to the Lower Pool.

17 Blackwall Reach looking towards Greenwich, 1750. Large East India Company ships usually moored at Blackwall, transferring their valuable cargoes into smaller craft for delivery to their City warehouses. To the right can be seen part of Philip Perry's Blackwall Yard, the largest private shipyard in the country. Blackwall Yard built over 100 East Indiamen and warships between 1612 and 1800, and repaired many more.

Sumptuous river-borne ceremonials have a history dating back to the early fifteenth century. Initially, both the Mayor and the City livery companies hired large barges, rowed by watermen, for a variety of festive occasions. In 1453 the Mayor, John Norman, had a barge built to carry him to Westminster to pledge his allegiance to the King, and began the tradition of the river procession. Accompanied by a growing number of specially built livery company barges, this annual procession transformed London's main highway into a grand theatrical spectacle.

Ceremonial barges also attended royal and public ceremonies and the opening of new bridges. Not only were there the splendid gilded and painted City barges, decked out with banners and scarlet-coated watermen, but all manner of other craft, floating tableaux and music. Both British and foreign commentators marvelled at these shows of corporate and commercial might, and likened London to Venice. Smaller scale events, such as regular regattas and races between professional watermen in their wherries, added other welcome touches of colour.

Large ceremonial barges were expensive to build, costing over £1,500 each by 1800. Most were constructed at Lambeth by shipwrights who specialised in building and repairing such barges. Between their outings, these valuable craft were normally laid-up in covered barge houses which lined the waterfront at Lambeth and Chelsea.

Although some livery companies were still building barges in the 1820s, river pageants became increasingly ill at ease with the overcrowded and dirty river of the mid-nineteenth century. In the 1840s, many livery companies gave up their barges, and in 1857 the City Corporation, who had just lost their conservancy responsibilities, abandoned the river procession to Westminster.

19 The City Corporation barge, 1804. Some 80 feet long, this craft, like other ceremonial barges, essentially had the lines of the much smaller watermen's wherries. Attending the barge are shallops, built to much the same design.

20 The Stationers' Company's last barge was built in 1826. The exaggerated stern gave the steersman a better view over the roof of the cabin. By this time, cabin roofs were usually railed to provide better accommodation for passengers and musicians. (right)

18 *Drawn elevation of the Goldsmiths' Company barge, dated 1776, by Richard Roberts, the Lamberth bargebuilder. (left)*

COURTESY THE GOLDSMITHS' COMPANY

23 *Carved and gilded figure of St Dunstan, which adorned the Goldsmiths' Company barge of 1744.*

COURTESY THE GOLDSMITHS' COMPANY

21 *'Order of Procession for the Barges' on Lord Mayor's Day, 1843. The Watermen's and Lightermen's Company was responsible for the arrangements.*

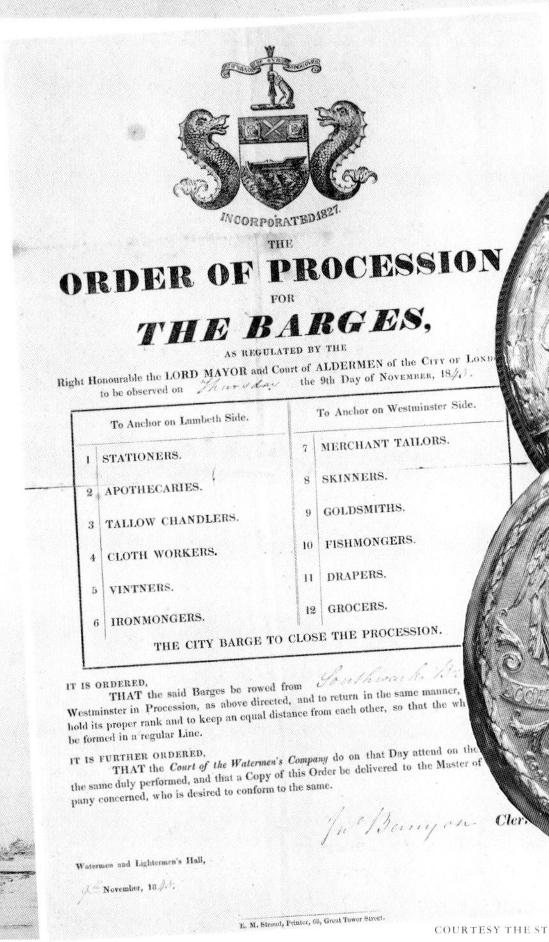

INCORPORATED 1827.

THE

ORDER OF PROCESSION

FOR

THE BARGES,

AS REGULATED BY THE

Right Honourable the LORD MAYOR and Court of ALDERMEN of the CITY OF LOND
to be observed on *Thursday* the 9th Day of NOVEMBER, 1843.

To Anchor on Lambeth Side.		To Anchor on Westminster Side.	
1	STATIONERS.	7	MERCHANT TAILORS.
2	APOTHECARIES.	8	SKINNERS.
3	TALLOW CHANDLERS.	9	GOLDSMITHS.
4	CLOTH WORKERS.	10	FISHMONGERS.
5	VINTNERS.	11	DRAPERS.
6	IRONMONGERS.	12	GROCERS.

THE CITY BARGE TO CLOSE THE PROCESSION.

IT IS ORDERED,
THAT the said Barges be rowed from *Southwark Br*
Westminster in Procession, as above directed, and to return in the same manner,
hold its proper rank and to keep an equal distance from each other, so that the wh
be formed in a regular Line.

IT IS FURTHER ORDERED,
THAT the *Court of the Watermen's Company* do on that Day attend on the
the same duly performed, and that a Copy of this Order be delivered to the Master of
pany concerned, who is desired to conform to the same.

Jno Benyon Clerk

Watermen and Lightermen's Hall,
9th November, 1843.

E. M. Stroud, Printer, 60, Great Tower Street.

COURTESY THE STATIONERS' COMPANY

COURTESY THE TALLOW CHANDLERS' AND GROCERS' COMPANIES

22 *Silver barge-masters' badges of the Grocers' (top) and Tallow Chandlers' (bottom) Companies. Barge-masters managed the barges and their crew.*

By 1800, opposition to dock building had diminished. When the West India Docks opened at Poplar, in 1802, they were London's first purpose built trading docks and the nation's greatest civil engineering structure. Their future was guaranteed by a valuable twenty-one-year monopoly on trade with the West Indies, tight security and fast turn-around of shipping.

The London Dock, opened at Wapping in 1805, enjoyed a twenty-one-year monopoly on all trade in tobacco, rice, wine and brandy, except that coming from the East and West Indies. In 1806, the East India Docks opened at Blackwall with a similar monopoly on far eastern trade.

South of the West India Docks the Corporation built and operated its City Canal. Opened in 1805, it provided a direct passage for shipping across the Isle of Dogs. Members and officers of the City Corporation were also involved with the management of the West India, London and East India Dock Companies.

New docks, basins and a canal were constructed on the Rotherhithe peninsula. In 1820 the Regent's Canal Dock opened at Limehouse. St Katharine Dock, opened in 1828, benefited from being closest to the City and from the termination of dock monopolies.

27 A busy quayside scene at the West India docks, 1830. (right)

28 Alderman George Hibbert, the first Chairman of the West India Dock Company. (centre, right)

29 The City Canal seen here before its closure in 1829. (far right)

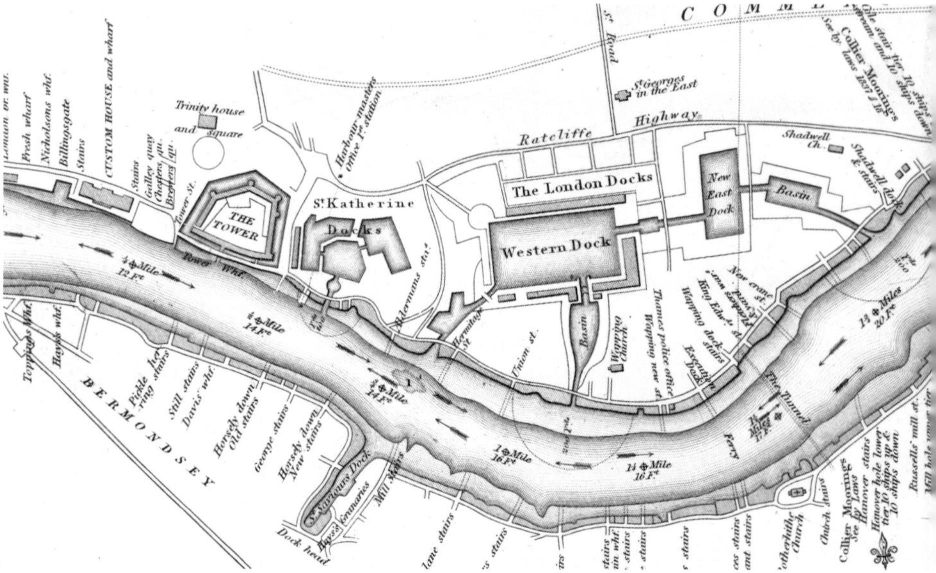

24

24 James Elmes' chart of the port records the extent of new dock building up to 1837.

25 Work at St Katharine's, 1827, reflects the enormous engineering achievements of the early docks. St Katharine Dock occupied the site of 1,250 houses. (top left)

26 The opening of Thomas Telford's St Katharine Dock on 25 October 1828. Crowds of spectators watch the 'Elizabeth', dressed with flags and her yards manned, enter the basin from the lock. (right)

30 The Commercial Docks, at Rotherhithe, seen from the east in 1813. Operated by three competing companies, the Rotherhithe docks concentrated on capturing London's important trade in timber and grain from the Baltic. (right)

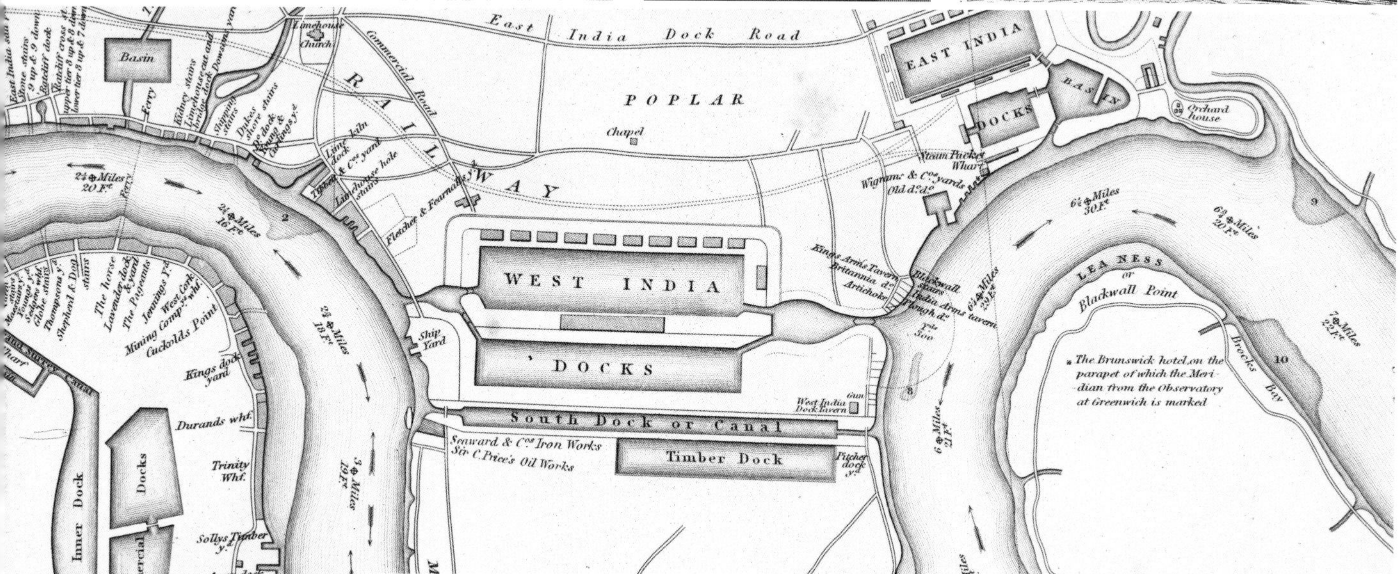
East India Dock Road
POPLAR
Chapel
Limehouse Church
Commercial Road
RAILWAY
Basin
EAST INDIA
DOCKS
BASIN
Orchard house
Steam Packet Wharf
Wigram & Cos yards
WEST INDIA
DOCKS
Ship Yard
West India Dock Tavern
South Dock or Canal
Timber Dock
Seaward & Cos Iron Works
Sir C. Price's Oil Works
LEA NESS
or
Blackwall Point
Brocks Bay
* The Brunswick hotel, on the parapet of which the Meridian from the Observatory at Greenwich is marked
Cuckolds Point
Kings dock yard
Durands whf.
Trinity Whf.
Inner Dock
Docks
Commercial
Greenland Dock
East Country Dock
Rotherhithe
Deptford
SURREY
KENT
Victualling Office
or the Red House

Despite the opening of the early docks, London's riverside wharves, especially those in the City, remained very active. Downriver of London Bridge, the wharves retained the shipping engaged in the coasting trade and much of that with northern Europe. Above the bridge, warehouses continued to be the focus of traffic with barges and small trading vessels.

By the 1850s the docks were in a weak position against the more centrally located river wharves. These wharves were now siphoning off three-quarters of the warehousing business of the docks, through barges which were allowed to come in and out of the docks, free of charge, to receive and deliver cargoes to ships. Increased free trade and an extension of Legal Quays and Sufferance Wharves strengthened their hand. The result was a wave of new warehouse building all along the river.

In the 1890s, fifty working wharves, including flour mills, lined the City waterfront. Backing up to Upper and Lower Thames Streets there were towering warehouses storing fruit, provisions, tea, wine, spirits, essential oils, spices, drugs, shells, furs, bristles, wool and carpets. Many of these warehouses also provided sales and auction services to City merchants.

31 The Blackfriars' waterfront, photographed from Blackfriars' Pier, around 1860. These wharves handled engineering equipment, coal, cement and corn.

34 With considerable artistic skill and lively imagination, Gustave Doré captured the scale of City warehousing in this view of Thames Street, 1872. (right)

32 Paul's Wharf and St Paul's Pier, 1884. The two nine storey buildings were operated by J J Smith & Co as a granary. (below)

36 The Upper Pool, around 1885. Beyond the lighters and watermen's skiffs, steam fish carriers and Dutch eel schuyts lie off Billingsgate Market. (right)

35 James Bunning's design for the Corporation's new Billingsgate Market, 1851. This fine Italianate building was itself replaced in 1874. (below)

33 The City waterfront seen from Southwark Bridge, around 1850. Completed in 1819, this bridge provided a valuable communication to the heart of the City. To the east, the river is busy with sailing barges, and paddle steamers are bound for Old Swan Pier. Alongside London Bridge is Fishmongers' Hall (1834) and beyond are the busy wharves of the Upper Pool. (below)

Despite the continued success of the riverside wharves, further new docks were built downriver. The Victoria Dock, designed for steamships, opened in 1855, with hydraulically operated entrance locks, links with London's railway system and its own telegraph service. The dock's instant success was followed by the opening of the Millwall Dock (1868), the Royal Albert Dock (1880), and Tilbury Docks (1886).

In 1909 the Port of London Authority was established to run the enclosed dock systems and manage the river, a function which the City Corporation had lost to the Thames Conservancy in 1857. The PLA carried out dock improvements, dredged the river channel for larger shipping, and opened the King George V Dock, in 1921, to make the Royal Docks the world's greatest dock complex.

By the 1930s the 'First Port of Empire' employed 100,000 people and handled 35 million tons of cargo within its 700 acres of enclosed dock water and at 1,700 riverside wharves. Most upriver warehouses remained active until the late 1960s, when containerisation led to the progressive closure of the upper docks.

37 Sailing barges at Southwark Corporation's Greenmoor Wharf refuse depôt, Bankside, around 1930. (above)
38 Dockers loading bags of Caribbean sugar into the North Quay Warehouses at the West India Dock, around 1930. Despite the limited introduction of mechanical handling, dockwork remained very labour intensive. (above, right)
39 Working on a ship's propeller at the King George V Dock dry dock, around 1930.

40 Carcasses of lamb being discharged onto the North Quay, Royal Albert Dock, around 1930. Since the closure of the upriver docks, the main port activity now centres on Tilbury Dock.
41 The City Corporation's Port Health Authority launch, the 'Howard Deighton', early 1930s. Port medical officers visited a large number of in-coming ships, on every tide, to check for infectious diseases.
39/40/41, top of page 15

42 Irongate Wharf and St Katharine Wharf, 1937. These were operated by the General Steam Navigation Company, which ran regular services to European ports. Behind the wharves, and to their right, are the warehouses of St Katharine Dock. (left)

43 The Upper Pool of London, March 1930. Rennie's London Bridge provided a splendid vantage point to watch the steamers berthed at the wharves, quayside activity, tugs towing barges and lighters being driven 'under oars'. The bascules of Tower Bridge (1894) opened around fourteen times each day, adding another exciting element. (right)

44 The meandering course of the Thames, from King's Reach to Greenwich Reach, is shown in this early aerial view of 1932. The river is lined with wharves, many of which could handle large ships. The St Katharine Docks and London Docks can be seen on the north bank past Tower Bridge. The roofs of the timber sheds of the Surrey Commercial Docks lie beyond, on the south bank, and in the distance is the Isle of Dogs.

Inside back cover (right, top)

Birds-eye view of the West India Docks, looking west from Blackwall, 1802. Although William Daniell accurately recorded the civil engineering of the docks, and the City Canal to the south, only the large range of warehouses on the North Quay were ever built on the scale depicted here. To maintain high security, the docks were protected by a ditch, a moat, and heavily armed militia.

COURTESY ANN WILSON

Inside back cover (right, bottom)

William Daniell's view of the East India Docks, Blackwall, looking south towards Greenwich, 1808. Opened in 1806, these docks incorporated John Perry's Brunswick Dock, with its great masthouse. Initially, cargoes were transferred from these docks to the East India Company warehouses in the City.

ACKNOWLEDGEMENTS

This booklet was published to accompany 'The Lord Mayor, the City and the River', a special exhibition at the Museum of London, June to December 1989. The Exhibition was sponsored by the Corporation of the City of London to mark the 800th Anniversary of the Mayoralty. The Museum of London acknowledges the help of the Port of London Authority, whose main picture collection it now manages. Much of the Museum's extensive collection of river and port material will be displayed at the Museum in Docklands planned to open in 1993.